FORWARD

Since THE GIFT OF THE WIND was written in the mid 1970's, countless copies of it have been shared with individuals who, in one way or another posed the magic question: "What is life all about, anyway?"

It seems, the same question occurred to Strong Elk and it led him on a journey which culminated in him choosing an all-encompassing purpose for his life different from the one he had accepted from the time of his birth. The individuals who have commented on THE GIFT OF THE WIND have indicated that it gave them insights into seeing themselves more honestly and clearly and, in many cases, it resulted in choosing a life purpose and aim very much different from the ones held prior to reading the manuscript.

Strong Elk discovered, as a result of his willingness to question all of his most cherished beliefs, that he had been living a very mechanical existence. As a result, he had been very much controlled by external circumstances and suggestions which, in his case, were very detrimental to living a serene, joyful and loving life. He decided that growth; wisdom and understanding were of greater value than the pursuit of comfort, pleasure, attention, approval, power and recognition. That growth, more often than not, required the exercising of physical, mental, spiritual and psychological muscles until such time as he was willing to surrender. Surrender to what? THE GIFT OF THE WIND may contain the answer to that question as well as the reason for doing so.

You are invited to join Strong Elk on his journey of self revelation. He is one man who was willing to risk everything to find his true, genuine self. For him the journey was worth it, necessary and unavoidable, since he saw that the concepts and beliefs he had lived by were, in fact, illusions which were life destroying. You may choose, after reading THE GIFT OF THE WIND, to also go on a journey of self-discovery to find the core of your being. If you do, you will meet many who are like Strong Elk along the way.

Have a pleasant and interesting journey.

Steinar

Note: All photos are of sculpture created by Steinar in fired and painted magic-clay. The cover photo is of a black walnut wood carving by Steinar.

TABLE OF CONTENTS

THE WISDOM
OF STRONG ELK

White Fawn, I now reflect in serenity on our wanderings and our existence and my being is filled with gratitude for we experienced the wonder of creation and achieved an understanding of the harmony of all things.

In silence, we learned to walk on the trail of the Spirit, to sit still in the presence of that which is eternal and to open our eyes to the beauty in all men. We saw the passing of the seasons and their cycles and understood that our seasons would also pass. We learned that joy and sorrow are but events of the moment to be accepted and appreciated for they equally contribute to the fullness of life.

We saw that the storms of our life cleanse us of our misunderstandings, as the storms of winter cleanses the earth so that new life may emerge. And, as the brightness of the sun is never greater than in the spring after the storms of winter, so it was after the storms of our life. In those moments of quiet we saw and felt new life awakening and our hearts were filled with the warmth of the sun.

We observed that as an eagle reaches its heights on the gift of the wind, so the winds in our life forced us to soar to the heights of our greater selves. We became thankful for the winds of adversity, for with each we found something of value in ourselves that had not been evident. We observed that our sleep was the death of a day and our awakening was each day new birth. We saw that to live in our minds in yesterday was not to live, but to waste life on that which had already died.

We learned that the yielding sapling would bend under the winds of the storm when the rigid oak would break under the same force. We learned to give into the wind until its force was spent and then continued to grow in the direction of the sun of our understanding.

We came to believe that each man has within him the power to rise on the gift of the wind. We learned that to shield our brothers from the wind was to do much harm, for it hampered their growth towards the sun of their understanding.

We came to believe that the aim in life is to grow towards our greater selves as the sapling grows into the tall tree. As Nature contributes to the tree's growth so the tree must contribute to Nature. It became our purpose to make our contributions to Life which had given us all.

And now, White Fawn, in the autumn of this journey, the time has arrived to pass these gifts on to those who could not sit with us in the warmth of our lodge and feel the wealth that comes from living in this understanding. As others contributed to our awakening with their words, it is now time to send our contributions forth.

CHAPTER 1

*DO NOT JUDGE YOUR BROTHER TILL
YOU HAVE WALKED A MILE IN HIS MOCCASINS.*

The burning sun was sinking towards the mesa in the West when I walked into the valley the old ones called "The Valley of Decision." It had been there many seasons before that I had plotted my course in life. I was returning again, after many summers and winters of wandering, to recapture and rejuvenate my dedication to that which is good and honorable.

The fire from the sun was scorching the sand beneath my moccasins and parching my lips. I walked slowly, scarcely emitting sound for I did not desire to disturb the quiet of this holy place. I walked towards the dark, green foliage surrounding the water hole the old ones called "Wisdom."

As I neared the water I heard splashing and I stole forward not knowing what man or beast might be partaking of the water's soothing coolness. On the bank opposite, I spied a soul thirstily drinking from the waters as if attempting to quench a lifetime of thirst in one moment.

I stepped from the bushes and said, "Greetings to thee, O' stranger." But the one did not acknowledge my presence, for the eyes and the heart of the stranger were lost in the despair of the past and impervious to those things and events by which the present is measured. Etched upon the stranger's face were the struggles of many alone moon and many suns of travel in bewilderment and confusion. From the appearance of the tattered leggings, the shredded loincloth and the torn moccasins, I discerned that nowhere along the way had there been time for rest and respite.

I knelt down, in silence, watching the stranger for a sign of awareness of my presence. In time he looked up and saw me. Again I approached the stranger with a greeting. "Where are you going and what is your path?"

He looked at me with eyes heavy from the burdens of life and said. "My path has been fashioned from the errors of youth. The canyon walls along the path and the steepness of the trail are so great that I cannot change my course. My journey leads me only towards that destiny non-forgiveness allows."

I sat for a moment digesting the fullness of the stranger's despair and, when with the silence I felt our spirits in tune, I ventured forth with another query. "Why, O' stranger, do you not shed the moccasins of the errors of your youth and take up new moccasins strong enough to carry your load without suffering and pliable enough to change your course?"

The stranger replied with an answer that both disturbed and startled me, for little had I realized how deeply the convictions were held. The one raised a leather covered leg so that I might see the droplets of blood escaping from the holes in the moccasins and said, "Many summers ago these moccasins were soft to the touch. They were strong enough to withstand the prodding of the sharpest rocks and they were nearly white from the care with which they were fashioned. However, with each erroneous step I took they became less pleasing to my sight, but also with each step they fit the contours of my feet better until now. My footsteps and my moccasins are insepa-rable. The path has now been decided. There is no one to fashion more comforting moccasins to replace these. "The one sighed heavily, stood up and turned towards the setting sun.

I shouted in desperation, "Wait!" and the stranger turned back towards me. Calling upon the spirit within me and with conviction of concern for the suffering of my brother, I start-ed to speak, "Once, I also traveled the trail you are now trav-eling and I made the journey toward that destiny called non-forgiveness. But along the way, I came upon someone wiser than I who had shed the moccasins of the errors of youth. The Wise One gave to me, out of love, a new pair of mocca-sins and helped me put them on. His words are still soothing to my ears and spirit. He said, 'Though the trail might be as steep and the rocks as sharp, with courage you will learn to be comforted by these new moccasins.' I followed his bidding and though the trail of life was equally as difficult, the load was lighter. No longer did the jagged rocks penetrate the leather and no longer did I stumble and fall for his hand reached out and steadied me, as my hand steadied him along the way."

The stranger looked at me, in puzzlement. I reached into my medicine bag and pulled out a new pair of moc-casins: fashioned from love, made with compassion and softened with the tears of life. I offered them and contin-ued to speak. "As the Wise One did to me so long ago, I would like to give you these moccasins of eternal hope.

Allow me to walk along the trail of life with you for a while, not to diminish your strength nor to carry that which is not mine, but to support you as you would support me. For a strong lodge is not made with one lodge pole, but several leaning on each other to give the whole structure much strength."

The one looked at me and in the eyes I saw a heart reaching. In silence, I called to the Great Spirit that the stranger might have the courage to pick up the moccasins I held forth. But hope waned in his eyes and my heart filled with sadness. I knew that my all was not sufficient to overcome that which had preceded me. The stranger turned towards the mesa that was aflame from the setting sun and walked away.

I gathered mesquite and used the flints from my medicine bag to start the fire that would warm me through the night. Darkness descended and out of the West, I heard the anguished screams of the stranger traveling on the path of non-forgiveness.

CHAPTER 2

THE WISE ONE

In the aloneness of the night that surrounded me, my thoughts drifted back to the beginning of my awakening and to the warrior who had reached out to me with a new pair of moccasins. It was at the moment of my darkest darkness that I was provided a way of understanding that changed the darkness to light, turmoil to peace and confusion to calm.

I had been counted among the bravest of the brave, the strongest of the strong, and the wisest of the wise. I had won many battles, gathered much wealth and many horses of my own. Mine was a stage of honor and recognition. My position was one of leader in my village. I had arrived at a point of seeing the fruition of all the dreams of my youth. I should have been filled with gratitude for I had achieved all those things. Then, at that moment as I looked back at my life; the many aims, the many struggles, the many battles, the many hunts, all the victories, all the honor and all the recognition I, Strong Elk, could see no meaning or purpose. Within my breast was an emptiness greater than that of the barren desert. In that moment, I was lost in confusion, lost in despair and lost in pain. Though I had all things, I realized I had nothing. It was at that time I decided to wander and to search in hopes of finding the answer to this emptiness.

I bid my wife, White Fawn, goodbye and set out from the village on foot and ventured into the mountains. I climbed to the high places above the nests of the eagles. I spent many suns alone in the stillness; a stillness that became more awesome than the stillness of a burial ground.

Through my search, my mind and thoughts were in turmoil. The questions without answers were without end. One question was supreme and encompassed all the others. "Why?" The response was always the same, a total nothingness.

I, Strong Elk, tell you these things so that you might understand my heart and beginnings. I tell you these things so you might know that I have lived the dreams of men and experienced the achievement of many things. I tell you these things so you might see that my emptiness came not from being without, but in spite of having many treasures, honors, and recognition.

On a night when there was no moon or clouds, while in a restless sleep, the Wise One appeared to me in a dream, a dream that was not a dream. The dream was the beginning of my awakening. I call him the Wise One though he has no name for he never revealed it. I had never seen him before, yet I knew him. I saw him in the night, sitting across the fire from me. He was very old and, yet, he did not appear old. His features were aged and marked; his hair was nearly the whiteness of winter snow; his eyes were steady, dark and deep. His carriage and posture was youthful, vibrant and strong. I have no way of knowing how he came into my presence.

"I have watched your wandering and struggle, Strong Elk. I have seen your search and confusion. I know of your victories and your honor. You have a great question, a question many of your brothers never ask. You also have the answer."

Though I relate his words, there was much that passed between us that was not of words. There came about an understanding beyond the scope of words, beyond the scope of my knowledge and beyond the scope of my experience.

I replied haltingly, fumbling for the proper response; words to impress, words to appease and words that would gain approval. I fumbled for courage, for pride, for dignity, but from my despair came my reply, "Wise One, if I had the answer, why would I search? If I knew, why would I be on this solitary journey? If I had found, why would I be lost?"

"Strong Elk, your journey, as it is for every man who searches for the truth, is a solitary journey. None can take this journey with you or for you. You are alone because only alone will you be awakened to that which you already know. You are lost because you are looking in the wrong places and wrong direction." He halted and though his words cut through me, as an accusation against an innocent one, they were spoken with gentleness.

He continued, "When one looks out there," he swept his hands from horizon to horizon, "one will never find the answer to your question. The ones out there will give many answers that appear to be the answers, but they walk in darkness as well, so their answers only create more confusion. To find your answer, Strong Elk, you must look within. You must look into the depths of your being. You must look at all you believe you are, all you believe you have to be, all you have lived by, fought for and done."

When I heard his admonitions, my life flashed before me. I saw many aims followed by success or failure, followed by emptiness after the triumph of success and approval. After failure, I saw guilt, anger and fear. I did not speak for the Wise One knew what was in my heart.

"I cannot give you the answer, Strong Elk. This you must find for yourself. But, I can give you some clues to guide you in your quest."

After several moments of silence, I begged, "Please give me these clues so that I might escape from this dark confusion that surrounds me."

He complied and began to speak.

"In the beginning, every man is awakened to life from the warmth of a mother's belly; a warmth of comfort and love that is without pain, without disapproval, without work and without want. All needs are provided without effort. It is a gift, this state of warmth."

He sat quietly while I digested his words and they were absorbed into my consciousness. Before I could question his words in relationship to my experience, he continued.

"You have this question, Strong Elk; perhaps you will hear my words. Perhaps the words of others will overpower what I share with you. I will speak only of my understanding and experience. You must decide for yourself to what extent we are brothers of the spirit. Listen not only to my words, but look also into your heart to see if we have a bond of experience and feeling. Many times, to find the truth, one must first search out the untruths. The answer to your question will be found in your past and not in the present or future."

He was, again, silent as if waiting for me to speak. I plead, "O' Wise One, my despair is great. Please help me to understand."

"I cannot help you, Strong Elk, for I can help no one. I can give only of that which has been given to me. These gifts are weapons to be used. I cannot shoot your bow for you nor throw your lance. If you choose to pick up these weapons, use them and practice with them, you will find much of interest. Many have I told of these things, but few have been willing to do the work, to put forth the effort of finding."

He looked into the night and his eyes left mine. His gaze went out as if into the distant past. For moments, the stillness was only broken by the crackling of the fire that warmed us. He started to speak again.

"When life is first breathed into the little one, his existence changes, his understanding begins. He becomes aware of and in contact with opposition. From a state of 'no wants' he enters life and his existence becomes centered on 'wants'. Without words, without teachings, without experience the little one begins to see and to value. In the mother's belly there were "no wants". He had come into this life. He had experienced something disturbing to his 'no wants' existence.

Now he wants to be warm, wants to be fed, wants attention, he wants love, he wants approval and he wants comfort. He does not want pain, hunger, cold, indifference, disapproval or struggle. So, this little one decides that to have 'no wants'; physically, emotionally, mentally and in his heart is to be his primary purpose for his life.. At every level of experience he demands 'no wants'. Because he had this state once as a gift, he now sees it as his right and he begins to search out all the ways to regain this state of 'no wants'."

He spoke slowly so I could follow each idea, each thought.

"Now, Strong Elk, if we follow this little one in his quest for the state of 'no wants' we will find answers to many things."

I waited patiently for the Wise One to continue his tale of understanding. My thoughts were on my search toward an answer, on the many answers I had heard to the many questions I had asked; on the answers that had appeased me for a moment, only to be followed by another question. The sound of the Wise One's voice ended my thoughts.

"This little one decides that in order to have 'no wants' he must have his way immediately with no opposition. The first way he sees to get his wants satisfied is to complain. So he begins to whine, to snivel and cry so that the whole world will stop and take care of his wants and, of course, his loving mother responds by doing everything in her power to make him comfortable. So, the little one decides that one way to get back into the state of 'no wants' is to complain. When the crying does not get results, he screams in anger for by now he is convinced that he is entitled to have his way and every one should stop what they are doing and respond to his wishes. The mother, now being disturbed herself by the screaming, attempts to appease the little tyrant by comforting him. The little one now understands, in his very being, that a way to have 'no wants' is to complain and if that does not get the response immediately, then he has rights and entitlements that will be responded to when he screams and kicks and is belligerent."

"Have you ever whined or sniveled to have your way, Strong Elk? And, if that didn't work, did you scream and raise your voice to demand that others do as you wished?"

The description of this little one was so vivid and demeaning. I wished to be above such behavior. I did not want to acknowledge that I, Strong Elk, a brave warrior would have stooped to adopting the behavior of a little one, but I had. Before any words of denial could come forth, through my mind flashed many pictures. I remembered relationships with White Fawn and others. I saw many times when I had not had my way immediately and I had become sullen and belligerent. I had withheld affection until my want had been satisfied. I saw the little one within me and the Wise One had not allowed me to escape from the truth of it. I lowered my eyes and nodded my head. I heard his laughter echoing through the mountains, yet it was devoid of mockery and full of knowing.

"Yes, Strong Elk, this little one is within you as he is within every man, but do not be discouraged. This little one can be rendered harmless and ineffective if you are aware of his presence. In fact, with a wise and understanding teacher to guide you, this little one within can be taught a new way of seeing…"

I had now become totally fascinated by the Wise One's tale, for it was pointing out much that I had not been able to see about myself. He began again.

"At a point, and this is different for every man, the mother realizes that the little one is beginning to control her life with his demands and his screaming. She sees that an intolerable situation is coming about. Now she begins to train and condition the child to fit in to the family and the tribe. She teaches him that he is not the only one with 'wants'. Through punishment or rewards, she teaches him that he must please her. If he pleases her, he is not disturbed and many times rewarded. If he displeases her, he is punished or denied some of his pleasures. This conclusion that he must please her extends to others as well. Now he has two opposing conclusions by which to have a state of 'no wants'. He does not see that to have his way without opposition and to do what others want him to do and please them are contradictory thoughts. He finds, further, that whether he has his own way or pleases others, he still has opposition. He still does not reach the permanent state of "no wants". This contradiction in him, which was created without words, will lead to turmoil and confusion in almost every act that he initiates.

"Strong Elk, have you ever attempted to please others to have your own way or to reach that state of your 'wants' being satisfied?"

Again the silence and again my mouth wanted to deny that I ever used these tactics of the little one. But, my life of relationships flashed before me and again I saw much that had been hidden from my awareness. I remembered the instances when the little one wanted to play, yet I had to gather firewood to escape punishment and have approval. I again felt the struggle within, at those moments. I saw the little one caught in confusion. The decision of playing and being punished or gathering the wood was difficult. Though, inadvertently, I opted for no punishment and received approval, my belly ached with anger and hurt. I also saw that as a youth, as a brave and as a chieftain, I had used this tactic many, many times and it had always created turmoil inside. I saw and felt all this and, again, I had to nod my head in agreement for the Wise One had locked me in with another truth.

"As this little one grows, Strong Elk, other factors and other people come into his existence. He begins to have 'revered ones" in his value system. He understands that certain ones within the tribe are looked up to: the mightiest chief, the medicine man, and the greatest hunter. Each intimates a reward for certain behavior and a punishment for other behavior and, most times, this is done in a very subtle manner. Without questioning the truth or values of these revered ones, he begins to follow blindly as his father did before him and his father before way back into the past. He has reached his fourth major conclusion: To do and act as suggested by the revered ones, for they offer many ways to reach that state of "no wants"; the forms of pain and pleasure changes from physical to intimations and suggestions within. These suggestions always offer rewards of approval, recognition and power over others. They hold out as punishment the ideas of disapproval, indifference and loss of importance. It becomes important to conform, without question, to the ideals of the revered ones.

"Now, the little one has four conflicting conclusions and methods to contend with in his quest for the state of 'no wants'. They are all incapable of helping him achieve the state he is attempting to return to, but he can't see this. He has now made himself a puppet of every suggestion of everyone he comes in contact with.

"Strong Elk, have you ever acted, without investigation into the validity of the actions, as you were told by these revered ones in an attempt to reach this state of 'no wants'?"

My inside screamed in anguish and pain. In that moment, I knew that I, Strong Elk, who thought himself a great warrior, had for a lifetime never had the answer to 'Why?' I saw that I had created an army of "non-persons" to help me attain that state of "no wants" but I was not the chief. They had become my many chiefs and I was the only warrior. All these things my heart understood, for I had seen. Another truth had been revealed to me.

"Strong Elk, when all these 'non-persons' have been unable to help the little one, who is no longer little, reach his aim, he reaches another conclusion. He decides that for him to reach the state of 'no wants', it is important for him to be different for his aim cannot be reached as he is. So he begins to lie to himself and create masks to hide his fear and anger. He pretends to be brave, he pretends to be noble, he pretends to be kind, however, all these masks and 'non-persons' are only facades to help him convince others to do his bidding and give him what he values the most which is total and complete fulfillment of all his 'wants'. Did you ever, Strong Elk, attempt to change someone else; to force them through suggestion or violence to be different so that you would again have 'no wants'?"

I could only nod in agreement. I realized that as I had grown in stature in the tribe, I had used all methods at my disposal to attempt to get others to change and become and do what I wanted them to be and to do. I had developed fear in others through suggestions. I had used my knowledge, my warrior's strength and my cunning to make others conform to my aims and desires.

I saw that the revered ones had used the same conclusions in their attempts to maintain and increase their control over others and me. I understood, in having the aim of "no wants", a warrior, chief or medicine man believes that he knows what is lacking in achieving this state, so the attempts to create the ideal fears so as to make his brothers conform. I saw this illness. I saw this in myself and in all those I had known through my life.

"The last act of this little-big one, when all these attempt at having 'no wants' have been frustrated, is to seek for the cause of this frustration. He begins to blame, he gets angry. He blames himself and accepts a state of guilt. If he can't find what or whom to make responsible, he becomes fearful. Once the little-big one has gone through this enough times, he becomes insecure. When a man is insecure he becomes very greedy and will use all kinds of means to insure the survival of all these non-persons who is not him, but they control all aspects of his life.

"This last act and conclusion of the little-big one, this looking for blame, leads to all the illnesses and wars of men. It leads to confusion, turmoil and hate.

"Strong Elk, have you ever blamed anything, anyone or anyplace for you state of wanting, your state of not being able to have 'no wants?'"

I was totally exposed. He had made it impossible for me to escape the responsibility for my acts and thoughts. Even as these conclusions of behavior were being presented to me, I was looking for the ones to blame, the ones who were responsible. I had to confess, then, to myself that I, Strong Elk, was responsible....no one else.

At that moment, the weight, which had been removed by seeing the non-persons within me, was replaced by the awesome thought that there was no answer to my question. I had the thoughts that existence was merely an accident, a sad joke. There arose a sense of hopelessness within me.

The Wise One continued to speak and I relate his words, for in my experience, since that night, I can verify that my perceptions changed. The weapons he gave me were powerful.

"If you have heard these words, Strong Elk, and if you are attentive each moment, you will begin to see differently. Much you have seen already, but this is only a beginning. You may find, as you observe yourself in relationships that you have in your life become the only one. You may see that you have come to believe that you have many rights and that these rights are yours only. You may learn to see this self-important, arrogant person, who lives with constant demands and expectations of life. You may see this warrior who behaves as a little one inside and outside. He dances to the drums of all those who promise pleasure in all its forms or threatens with pain and punishment in all their forms. You may learn to see that all those things you consider your strengths and your values are, in fact, your weaknesses and they destroy your potential for peace and harmony. You may find that these values, these ideals that have guided you to this point, are but many 'non-persons' who control you and keep you in bondage. You may see that all you think you are is a puppet to every thing that happens to you. You may see all these things and understand these things, if you have reached the point of willingness to test that which you think you are against that which you might be."

All these things he said slowly, so that each thought traveled through my mind several times before the next statement was presented. He stopped speaking and looked into my eyes with a gaze open and at peace. There were no questions in his heart, for he had a sense of acceptance about him. My thoughts had now examined his words and I began to question.

"Wise One, I can see these things or some of these things. I can see this little one in me and many 'non-persons' of my creation. I can see this puppet that dances to the drums of suggestions. But, this still does not give me the understanding that will fill my heart and remove the emptiness within. I still do not know, why?"

He replied, "These things of which I speak are a beginning only. There is much more that will come to you if you persevere. I have given you weapons of understanding and as you become proficient in their use, other truths will become evident. Much of what will become evident will take place when you learn to accept the events of life instead of attempting to force life into the image of an ideal. Much will become evident when you learn to stop the battles within, when the one within becomes stronger and takes away the power from the 'non-persons' who have and are controlling you.

"It takes time, Strong Elk, but, more than time, it takes courage and willingness to go through the pain of growing towards that which you are. Be patient. Others will come who will present other truths for you to examine."

I was again alone in the night. I did not see him depart. I felt calmness within, for I knew I had experienced the end of one life and the beginning of another.

CHAPTER 3

THE GIFT OF THE WIND

The Wise One had given me much to contemplate. In that solitude, above the nests of the eagles, before the snows of winter had begun their descent into the valley below, I began, from the wisdom given to me, to find that which I had been seeking.

As I pulled out the little one within me and examined the motives beneath all the actions of my life, the motives that had created all the non-persons who had ruled my life, I discovered in my inner self only one motive. This motive was, as the Wise One had expressed, to live with "no wants", no opposition to my wants and wishes, to have no resistance, to have no interference.

I came to realize, through observation of the little one within that in my mind, the gift of "no wants" I had experienced in my mother's belly had been altered. The gift of "no wants" in the mind and heart of the little one had become an entitlement, a right.

Through looking within, I saw this first conclusion of having a right to have "no wants" had led to the conclusion of having many rights. Each right was an ideal. Each ideal had to be defended. Each ideal came into conflict, not only with the ideals of others, but also with contradictory ideals within myself. I saw that others based their ideals on what they believed to be their rights. These rights, these ideals, these often unobtainable absolutes had become the source of much conflict in my life.

Not until the outward aims had been realized did I accept and experience the nothingness that led to the searching for a different answer to my purpose of existence. It became obvious that the idea of having "rights" to "no-wants" was not the legitimate purpose of my life. But, then, if the striving for "no-wants" was not the aim, what was?

My mind traced and retraced all the steps of my life, yet the answer was not forthcoming. I was becoming exhausted from the many suns of concentration and the struggle became a torment for I could not see this elusive answer.

After a night of deep sleep, I awakened with the sun, and I walked to an outcropping of rock. I climbed upon it and looked about me. I saw the forest to the East, the valley below, the plains to the South and the snow-covered peaks to the North. I sat down on a ledge and marveled at the vastness of creation.

I felt the warmth of the sun dissipating the chill of the night. I saw the clearness of the sky and far below I saw the mist covering the valley floor. In the white mist, I spotted a moving dark speck. I felt the wind blowing through my hair and heard the rustling branches of the trees swaying to the same breeze that caressed me.

My eyes became fixed on the dark spot in the mist and I followed it as it moved. I do not know how long I sat there watching. Slowly, the speck grew larger until I could recognize the outline of the wings of a bird. I noticed that the bird was rising towards me. It was not struggling to rise. It was not exerting effort to rise. Its wings seemed not to move. Presently I recognized the proudest of all birds, the eagle. I marveled at its smoothness in flight. I became aware, through ever so slight movements of its wings, it would ascend higher and higher and it kept growing in size. I wondered at this strange ability to rise without struggle, without conflict, without apparent effort.

Suddenly, while observing, a realization came to me. It was at first just a glimmer; a trace of awareness. The eagle rising towards me, together with the wind through my hair and the swaying of the branches of the tree made me see that the noble eagle was using the gift of the wind. It was using the resistance of the wind against its body to rise to heights that the strength of its wings could not carry it.

My mind became agitated and excited, for some darkness of misunderstanding was leaving me. I thought: If the aim of existence was not to arrive at a stage of having "no wants", could it be possible that the true aim is to rise to the heights of the eagle and higher? If the true aim was to be that of reaching the heights of my greater self, to make the one within explore all the potentials given, then, perhaps the greatest gift, indeed the greatest need, was to have resistance of the wind and use it as did the eagle.

In the light of the morning sun, I felt a well of brightness within. I felt a light dispelling a part of the inner darkness.

My conclusion when I left my mother's belly was to have as an aim, my only life's aim, that of reaching again that state of "no-wants." On that outcropping of rock, above the nests of the eagles, while looking at the vastness of creation, while seeing the rising of the eagle, while feeling the wind against my body, a question came to me as if some other voice was speaking. But, I knew the voice came from within. The voice said, "Strong Elk, you have tried your aim and it left you wanting. Perhaps the Creator of all things has a different aim for you. Look at his creation and see the common bond of all living things. If you can see the purpose in the smallest thing, you may see the purpose, the aim, the creator has for you."

This voice stopped me. It shut off much confusion. It removed many questions. It left but one question. What is the Creator's aim and what could I, Strong Elk, do to fulfill this aim?

I knew then that my course was set for me. I understood that my true finding had begun. I stood up and turned from the view of the valley and the eagle. As I jumped from the rock, I stumbled and fell. The hard ground stunned me. For many moments I lay still. As my eyes focused, I saw in front of me a fragile little shoot of a tree. It was so delicate that I could have ripped it out with little effort, yet it had escaped to light of day, through the hard ground that had just stunned me. Towering above me was the mother of this fragile shoot. It was a proud strong tree. I looked at it and again at the shoot.

That towering tree had once been a seed, yet it had reached its present size. How?

I felt the solid, hard, unforgiving soil beneath me and I knew how. That magnificent stature had been realized and given strength only through the effort of breaking through the resistance of the soil.

Understanding came quickly then. The Creator's aim for that seedling was to provide the opportunity to grow into a massive tree, to have the strength to support its many branches. To reach its heights, it had needed the resistance of the soil as the eagle needed the gift of the wind to reach its greater heights. Without the resistance and the willingness to use that resistance, neither the shoot nor the eagle would have reached their true purpose. The eagle would have been a dove and the tree would have been a blade of grass. More excitement crowded into my mind. Thoughts raced to formalize this understanding. Questions and answers came rapidly.

If the aim of the Creator is for the shoot to become a tall tree and if the aim of the Creator is for the eagle to rise above all other birds, and if man has been given more gifts than all other creations, then to what heights does the Creator aim for man to reach? If the eagle needs the gift of the wind and if the tree needs the gift of the hard soil to reach their highest potentials, then what manner of resistance does man need, as a gift, to reach the destiny for which the Creator designed him?

I laughed out loud. I jumped with inner joy. I shouted with glee for all the creatures around me to hear. I had found the greatest gift and never before understood its value. I had complained about it and attempted, in all my efforts, to escape from it. This most precious gift that the eagle used and the shoot of the tree used, I, Strong Elk, had never acknowledged as a gift. I saw that this force against my desire to have "no wants" was the only tool provided for me, or my brothers, to use to grow towards our greater destiny.

The thrill I experienced with this understanding filled me with laughter. I knew then, by seeing the wind and the soil and all opposition as gifts; by appreciating this force, this resistance, I could begin to use it as the eagle uses the wind. I could stop struggling within and without, for I would never be able to escape it. I could accept it for it was a part of the plan of the Creator. I would begin to ascend to my highest potential for I had recognized this most valuable gift.

Again I re-examined my total existence with the eyes of one who understood the gift of the wind. I saw many aims that I had struggled for and I saw many resistances. I saw with each aim there had been a force against or in opposition to the fulfillment of my aim. I saw with each resistance, I had either chosen to give up or work through it so as to achieve my aim. When I had worked through the resistance, I had grown, learned and gained an experience of value. I had become a strong warrior not by wrestling with children, but by wrestling with stronger warriors. To develop, I had needed a force stronger than I to oppose me.

During this inner search, I understood that those who opposed me and those who resisted my aim were, in truth, my greatest allies. They forced me into untapped areas of my being for the strength and ability to fulfill my aim. In this realization I, Strong Elk, released from my heart the resentments, the angers and the hates I had carried towards all those who had been a force against my wishes of having "no wants". I forgave them, as I forgave myself. I realized I also had been a force against the many aims of many of my brothers and to overcome my force, they too had to reach within for their greater strength.

My time in the high places had come to an end. In the aloneness, I had been given the freedom from the bondage of the many "non-persons" who had controlled my life. I had been given the freedom from the foolish conclusions of the little one. I had been given, by a different aim, the freedom to experience the gift of the wind without attempting to run from or avoid it. I could now begin to explore my greater destiny.

CHAPTER 4

WHAT I AM MUST BE SUFFICIENT
FOR WHAT I AM NOT HAS DIED.

From the point of despair that had encompassed me when my pilgrimage into the high places had begun, I had arrived at a feeling of well-being. I felt a healing taking place inside. As the Wise One had stated, "To find a truth, one must go back to the beginning and find the un-truth." As I had recognized and released the "non-persons" who were not I; I had begun to see the one within who had been burdened and chained for my whole life.

I saw, I was not the greatest warrior. There were many others braver than me, stronger than me, more cunning and more able than me. I saw that these warriors who had powers beyond mine, had become revered ones to copy and emulate. I saw that their taunts and suggestions had been accepted as ideals, as idols for me to strive towards. I saw the struggles and the fear as I had attempted to hide all things of me that did not conform to those ideals and idols.

Everywhere I looked in my life, in every area, I saw idols and ideals handed down to me by others, accepted as valuable by me without investigation or validation, fought for, sustained and pushed into prominence in my life. I saw, with each "non-persons", each suggestion and each accepted idea, the one within had died a little. The voice of the one within had been silenced by the clamor and confusions created by all the "non-persons". I saw my creation of these non-persons had caused emptiness, separateness and aloneness. And, as I saw these things, the one within began to become visible to me.

Before I reached the valley floor, I smelled the wood-smoke from many cooking fires. I heard the barking of the dogs and the laughter and shrieks of the children at play. I felt a great comfort. For the first time in many winters, I had a feeling of belonging. Yet, I knew that I did not have a need to belong, for I was empty no more.

As I entered our lodge, White Fawn silently greeted me with a smile. In her eyes I saw wonderment and a gratitude for my safe return. As I looked from the smile on her lips to her eyes, she lowered them for it was a custom of our tribe that a woman must not challenge the gaze of a warrior. I saw, again, bondage. White Fawn was, as the one within me had been, in bondage to a lifetime of suggestions placed upon her by the non-persons of her existence. Though her heart may have wanted to express many things, it was impossible to do so. All the many winters of being told of forbidden things had silenced the one within White Fawn as well.

I seated myself on the buffalo robes opposite her and smiled. I had no words. I did not know how to begin to tell her of my experiences. Again she raised her eyes to mine and I saw a question forming in her thoughts.

"Welcome, Strong Elk, did your wandering provide that which you were searching for?"

"Many of the things of my greatest longing were pro-vided on this journey, White Fawn." I replied. "Many things must I tell you, for many things are in my heart. I must tell you these things for you are a part of me, a part of my heart, so you must also have this knowledge."

"I know there is a hunger, Strong Elk. Let me prepare the meat of the deer for your nourishment and strength then we will talk of these things."

I nodded approval and gracefully White Fawn moved to the entrance of our lodge. As she went out, she created a silhouette against the light of the entrance and I remembered many winters of struggles from the time she had been a maiden of much laughter. A feeling of knowing that through the struggles a bond had been created that was a totality unto itself. And, yet the bond I saw was perhaps created by two "non-persons", sustained by two non-persons and built by two "non-persons". My fear again touched me. I wondered if this bond would still be there after I had allowed the one within me to be exposed to her awareness.

White Fawn returned to my side and placed before me the warm food I had been without since my departure from the village. She sat quietly by my side as I ate. I chewed slowly and allowed my heart to open up to the spirit in the lodge. To sit in silence without thought, without inner war and allow the essence of the lodge to touch me was a feeling unlike any I had ever experienced. I could have shouted with joy or shed tears of gratitude for everything was close to me and a part of me.

When finished with the meal of warm food, I stretched out and beckoned for White Fawn to lie down beside me.

She placed her head on my chest and I embraced her. She lay silent for a while and then began to speak.

"I feel, in your heart you have changed, Strong Elk. There is about you a peace, where previously there was anger, frustration and disgust. You are different from the warrior who left my side to wander. Will you now tell me of these things that have changed you?"

The gentleness in her voice soothed me. This woman who had been with me since the twilight of my youth and who now breathed lightly on my chest, was about to hear my confession of awareness.

I began, "White Fawn, you who stood by me through all the battles, I will tell you of my greatest battle, a battle in which I am not yet victorious, but I know in my heart that I will be.

"Many things have I done and many things I have been. In the being and doing of those things that you know as Strong Elk, I lived a lie. I lived with deceit. I mislead you and everyone into a false belief of who I am." I stopped, for it was difficult for me to find the words that she would understand. Though she had questions, she was silent and I continued.

"White Fawn, you have never known the real me within. I have never allowed you to see beneath my masks and my costumes. Not once have I allowed you close enough to see and touch me as I truly am."

She responded to my confession and her words were wisdom.

"Strong Elk, as a young maiden when I first gazed upon you, I saw the one I was to love for my whole life through. You were not aware of my eyes upon you nor of the moment my love for you made itself known. You were alone by the river. I was walking toward the river when I first saw you. You had your bow tightly drawn with an arrow in place and your aim was steady. If you had let the arrow fly, it would have found its mark in the heart of a doe grazing peacefully. I held my breath, waiting for you to release the arrow. But, you lowered the bow and allowed the doe to graze without harming her. At that moment tears came to my eyes and my heart filled up with love for you."

I did not understand how this could be and I questioned, "How could love become alive by watching me not kill the doe?"

"I saw you, Strong Elk. I saw a gentle one who would lower his bow to allow life rather than to take life and so gain honor from the tribe. I saw, you had much caring, consideration and thoughtfulness. I saw, though you were strong and had much power, what I valued was this gentleness and willingness to do no harm. This was the warrior I saw. This was the one whose children I wanted to bear, the one who could make my eyes fill up with tears of gratitude by just being."

I squeezed her tightly and my fears and anxiety left me, for she knew the me within. She continued to speak.

"Strong Elk, I have always known the one deep within

you. Many times you have tried to hide for you were afraid, but I saw you lower your bow, knew this covering was for the expectations and benefit of others. I was not deceived. Many times I wondered if you would ever allow the one within to exist openly so that I could express all that is in my heart. I have waited a long time. I saw in your face, when you returned from your journey, my wait was over. I have much love for you, Strong Elk, as I know you have much love for me."

In the warmth of our lodge, I experienced for the first time the warmth of two hearts beating to the same inner voice. I, Strong Elk, wept as White Fawn wept. We had found each other through the clamor of all the "non-persons" who had ruled our lives.

This, then, was the first experience of what happened to me when I stopped being that which was not me. The one by my side had sat patiently waiting for the one within to become brave enough to reveal himself openly.

CHAPTER 5

THE GIFT OF FREEDOM FROM FEAR

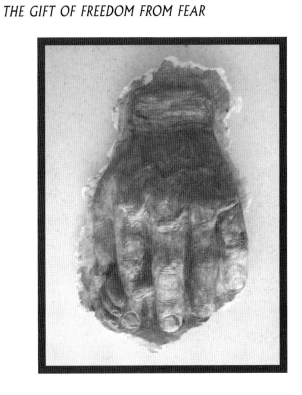

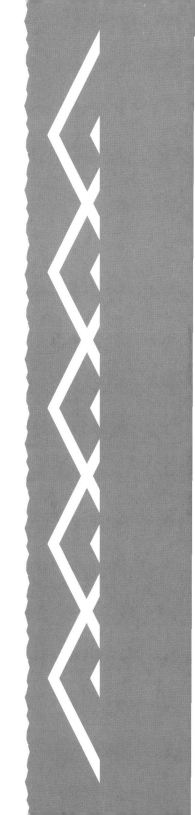

After I returned from my journey, I immersed myself in living within the tribe. I had the opportunity, through new eyes, to observe many things. These unclouded eyes were able to see beneath the many masks of my brothers. Beneath the masks I saw fear. In seeing and accepting the fear, I began to understand it.

I began to acknowledge my own fears. I examined the fear which had hung over me as I anticipated White Fawn's reaction to my discoveries. In my mind, I took fear apart and found it to be fascinating. In looking at the fears of my brothers and the fears I had experienced, I discovered there was only one fear, the fear of not surviving. I saw, fear was not tangible but the creation of my thoughts. Fear came to my mind because I did not know the certainty of the outcome of some future event. My mind and the "non-persons" made many horrible suggestions as to the outcome that my body reacted to as if this was real. Through my life, I had wanted this assurance that tomorrow I would have "no wants". My experience had taught me that in my life I had never been at this stage, but in my heart the "non-persons" proclaimed it as my right. With the expectation of having this right fulfilled came the fear of not getting it. I understood, from my journey back from the high country that my expectation of acceptance by White Fawn, and my not-knowing, had led me to experience this distur- bance inside which is fear. I saw this wanting and I realized that I had no guarantee of the fulfillment of my want and, through this, I had imagined many things opposed to the realization of my aim and in the imagining was fear.

Fear, then, was a result of many "non-persons" in me who were striving for acceptance, approval and recognition. The realization of not knowing was creating results in my mind before the event took place. Fear was the prompting by all the "non-persons" telling my mind, if this and if that. These "ifs" of the "non-persons" and the pictures they created were illusion. These "ifs" were an assumption accepted in the mind, but my body, which was directed by my thoughts and feelings, had no way of knowing that these "ifs" were assumptions. So, my body reacted as if the assumptions were real.

I remembered an event of fear that had taken place before my youth. I had been deep in the forest and darkness had descended before I realized how far away from the village I had wandered. I stumbled through the dark and as the night closed me in, I became aware of sounds. I could not see where the sounds were coming from. I heard the hooting of an owl in the distance and somewhere ahead of me the barking of dogs. I headed in the direction of the sound of the dogs for I knew they were the dogs of my village. As I proceeded I heard more and more sounds and these sounds I could not recognize. My heart began pounding faster and faster. I could hear it beating in my ears. My body tensed and my eyes traveled everywhere, though all I could see were outlines and shadows.

I heard the sharp crack of the breaking of a twig and I

froze. Every part of me wanted to run, fight, or scream, but I did not know what to fight or run from and I could not scream, for I knew that this was not proper or fitting to do. (I had been told this over and over until I believed it.) My whole body was in such a state of tension that, even now, I can feel the muscles of my belly tightening up. At that moment, my thoughts took over; the "non-persons" began to prompt me. "What if it is a war party sent out by some enemy of my people? What if it is a bear? What if it is a timber wolf?" In a flash I saw myself scalped by the enemy of my people, mauled by a bear and dragged off by a wolf. My mind did not know this, but my body reacted as if it was real.

Out of the night, from the direction of the sound of the snapping twig, I heard the voice of my uncle calling, "Strong Elk, where are you?"

I relate this for it was an event of fear, an event of sheer terror, yet none of my imaginings took place. My body had reacted to fighting or running from signals sent by the suggestions of the "non-persons" who were in a state of not knowing. Yet, what was real was that I had no reason to fight or run, for there was nothing harmful around me.

In my examining fear, it began to take on strange shapes and it came into evidence in many forms. The "non-persons" called warrior had this feeling when he allowed his thoughts to paint pictures of losing in the battle, though the battle had not yet begun. The body reacted as if death was already nearby. The hunter had this feeling before or during the hunt, when he allowed the mind to paint pictures of the inability to find game or hit the mark. The wife had this feeling when in the process of cooking, something went wrong and her mind painted a picture of the anger of her husband.

All these pictures; all this fear came about because to lose the battle, not be successful in the hunt or to not be the perfect wife would tarnish or destroy the image demanded of that particular "non-person". All these "non-persons" who demanded perfection, who demanded a state of "no wants" painted pictures of punishment or doom and the body reacted as if this doom, this failure, and this punishment were already being administered.

I understood that fear, all fear, was not real. There was no solution to fear for the mind had only created a picture and not the actual thing. There was no solution for me, at that moment in the forest to the attack of a bear, a wolf or a war party. I could do nothing for the objects of my fear did not exist in my experience at the time. I could not run from a bear that was not there. I could not fight a war party many suns travel away from me at that time.

This thing called fear, then, is never based on reality, though the body reacts to it as if it is real. This fear always deals in the future. It is very illusive, for it tricks one into at-tempting to handle situations it presents to one now and, yet, we cannot live tomorrow today. We cannot live the night until we have gone through the day.

As a warrior, I had the occasion to be attacked by a bear while I was not in a state of alertness. When the real bear attacked, my body and my senses reacted impeccably and I killed it. When the real bear attacked there was no fear, there was only action. I saw this in the examining of fear.

Through this searching I received another gift: The gift of the freedom from fear. I became aware that the now was the only reality. This instant, this moment, was the only moment I could do anything about. Having lived through many moments, I saw I had always been around after the moment; the challenge and the situation had passed.

Also, I accepted, I would always be in a state of not knowing and this not knowing kept me alert to the wonders of my experiences. I began to embrace this not knowing for it was true living. I found, through examining fear; to know, to have certainty, is to close the doors on opportunity. To know or be certain lulls one into a sleep which makes one misinterpret events and be unprepared.

CHAPTER 6

WHEN A MAN SEES HIMSELF AS A REFLECTION
HE CEASES TO BE THAT WHICH HE IS...

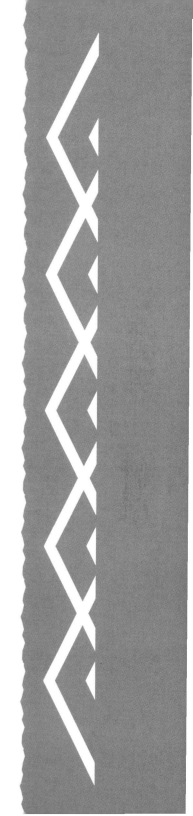

A great awareness came to me while fishing with Spotted Wolf. He was a young brave of many talents and much promise. He was recognized as a future chief for he showed the qualities necessary for leadership. The other young braves looked up to him and many young maidens looked at him with longing.

Before the break of day, we had set out in a solitary canoe to spear the fish before the winter ice covered the waters. The mist hung heavy along the shoreline of the lake, as we pulled the canoe through the waters. The lake was smooth and still, the blanket of mist made the chill air heavy and I shivered from the dampness as I guided the canoe.

I looked at Spotted Wolf kneeling in the bow of the canoe and marveled at the smoothness and power displayed by this young man. I became fascinated by the action of his paddle as he rhythmically dipped it into the water, pushed the water back, and lifted the paddle out of the water to again begin the motion downward. I saw the reflection of the paddle in the waters and then the reflection and the paddle merged into one. It seemed as if the reflection and the water did not want to separate from the paddle for they clung to it until Spotted Wolf had lifted it high out of the water. It appeared as if the image of the paddle wanted to become a part of the paddle, to have substance with it.

As our canoe rounded a point of land, the mist parted

and our eyes beheld a beauty and a stillness of great sensation. The tall pines reaching for the heavens also reached into the depths of the water. Seeing solid land and the land reflected in the lake made us cease the paddling. We allowed the canoe to drift without disturbing the image.

A lone hawk circled the lake above us and its sudden shriek pierced the quiet morning, protesting our intrusion into its domain. The shriek awakened us from our reverie.

Spotted Wolf turned towards me and questioned, "Will we spear many fish today, Strong Elk?"

"That is our hope. We will be successful if we are favored with patience, alertness and determination. First, we must find a place acceptable to our purposes. You must use your heart and your knowledge to guide us to this place."

As I answered, I wondered which direction Spotted Wolf would choose to go. He looked puzzled for an instant, but he made his decision quickly, as though he knew where the fish would be found. He motioned toward a small island a short distance away and in unison we moved the canoe toward it. As we neared our destination, Spotted Wolf motioned for me to slow the canoe down. He replaced the paddle with a fish spear. He held the spear loosely and as we neared the shoals his body tensed as he caught sight of a fish. I moved the canoe ever so slowly in the direction of his gaze. Presently a large fish came into view, heading towards us from the side. I lost sight of it as it passed into the reflection of Spotted Wolf. I watched him look into the water as he followed the movement of the fish and at the instant he threw his spear, his eyes shifted to the reflection of himself. There was an unnatural movement in his thrust. His spear did not hit the mark.

I saw anger and shame come over him, for he knew, in his heart, that it was an easy mark. He exclaimed his disgust and anger. I waited until the force had subsided before speaking.

"Spotted Wolf, I have learned a great lesson from you today and I hope you have learned the same." I made the statement without any intent to ridicule.

"Do not taunt me, Strong Elk. I missed the fish and I should not have. It angers me for you are laughing at me."

"I am not laughing at you, Spotted Wolf. You missed the mark, but that is not uncommon. In the course of the day, we will miss the mark more often than we will hit it. What is important is that you see why you missed in this instance. Why do you think you missed, Spotted Wolf?"

"I do not know. It was such an easy target, yet I missed it." He replied.

"I have seen you miss the mark many times without getting angry. This time you became angry where, in other instances, you accepted the miss without anger. Why did you get angry?" I questioned again.

"I became angry because; it was foolish for me to miss."

Spotted Wolf remained silent and I continued.

"I shall tell you what I observed, for in this event is

much wisdom and understanding. I observed a warrior perfectly trained to spear the fish, a warrior with all the ability, accuracy and strength to be successful in this situation. Yet, he failed, why?"

"Your eyes were on the fish. You were alert and you were tensed to strike. I saw your eyes leave the fish. You were distracted. You made your thrust without having your eyes on the fish. Do you know what distracted you? Do you know why this time you became angry?"

Spotted Wolf searched his mind and though he knew the truth, he could not admit it. He could not face this non-person within him who had caused him to miss the mark. He lowered his eyes and shook his head meekly.

"I don't know why I missed, Strong Elk."

"Perhaps you will be angry with me for the things I will reveal to you. Understand what I say is not meant to anger you. I say it to awaken you to the seeing of a force that hinders all men in their attempts to hit the mark of their aim. The quiet waters demonstrated a great lesson, a lesson that would have been difficult to see otherwise. Let me explain.

"As the fish swam towards you, I could see it clearly, but when it came close I lost the sight of it. Your reflection covered the water. As you were ready to throw the spear, your eyes also saw your reflection and you were distracted from your aim. What distracted you? Did the reflection? The reflection could have distracted you, but I think not. What

distracted you was pride and vanity which the reflection represented."

He thought for a moment and I knew that he struggled
within. I waited and finally he spoke.

"I acknowledge that my eyes saw my reflection and this
caused me to miss the mark. However, I do not understand the
vanity and pride of which you speak."

"Recall deeply the thoughts in your mind. They were
fleeting thoughts accompanied by fleeting feelings and very
difficult to pin down. See the reflection. The reflection is
nothing, but it represents something. What does the reflection represent?

"You see a young brave in the water. What are the attri-
butes of a brave and a warrior? What are his skills? Can you
see what the reflection represents? Can you see what ideal
it represents? Can you see your mind upon recognizing the
image, telling you that in spearing the fish the warrior would
be impeccable? He would be smooth and powerful. Did your
mind tell you that this perfect act would bring you the reward
of approval and recognition you crave, that I would relate the
tale of your ability to the tribe?"

Spotted Wolf sat sullen and withdrawn, for I had cut him
deep. This lesson, this experience could not be left to dissipate
like the mist in the morning sun.

"Many times, Spotted Wolf, I have missed the mark when
I should have hit it. I have searched back into the moments

and found much that angered me, for I saw the true reason I missed. I missed each time when I became aware of a reflection that demanded perfection. I looked at this reflection in my own eyes or in the eyes of others and when I became aware of it, something inside me kept me from concentrating on the act. I concentrated instead on the results or the rewards of performing the perfect act. When I saw myself as a reflection, I stopped being that which I am and attempted to become that which the image demanded. I lost, in that instant, the naturalness necessary to be successful in the act."

"I am hearing your words, Strong Elk, and I am trying to understand. Are you saying, when my mind becomes aware of my eyes viewing myself or the eyes of others viewing me, this awareness prevents me from acting freely?"

I smiled, for Spotted Wolf had understood and I continued.

"That is precisely what I am trying to show you. This awareness, the desire to fulfill the demands of the image and the craving for approval and recognition creates a bondage that prevents us from allowing the natural one within us to perform up to his abilities. If we can learn to recognize these reflections only as images just like the reflection in the water and dismiss them from our minds, then we can proceed towards our target unhindered."

Spotted Wolf smiled sheepishly and spoke.

"I feel very foolish for having been distracted. It was very painful for me to miss the mark when you were watching me. I shall try to heed this lesson and not allow reflections and images to control and distract me from my aims."

"Spotted Wolf, you have much ability and you will become a great warrior. I know this as you know it. This lesson is, for you, the beginning of your opportunity to take charge of your destiny. Be willing to ignore the reflections for they will hamper your quest."

I set our course with the motion of my paddle and we again set forth in pursuit of fish.

CHAPTER 7

THE GIFTS OF HAPPY HAWK

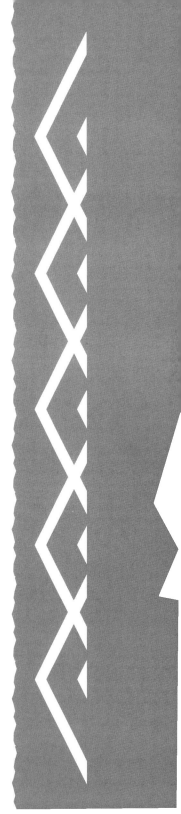

Many moons after the beginning of my new life, I was privileged to encounter one who laughed much and had a countenance that radiated joy. He was a warrior with a spirit more free than the birds in the skies.

I was on a hunt for the meat that would be dried by White Fawn for winter storage. I was deep in the forest. The wind was at my back for I had not yet begun the stalking of the deer. As I broke through a thicket, I entered upon the camp of a warrior from an unfamiliar tribe. He was facing me and I held out my hand in the sign of peace. He did likewise.

In the tongue of my people I offered an apology, "Forgive me, strange warrior, I did not intend to intrude into your camp."

He looked at me and his face showed puzzlement. He then smiled. I did not think he understood my tongue. I spoke again, "Forgive me. I did not intend to cross into a camp that was not mine."

He replied in the tongue of my people however, the words were formed with some difficulty.

"Mine! Mine! Nothing is mine. I do not understand 'Mine' I do not understand 'yours?'" He laughed.

I attempted to explain with words and gestures. I pointed to his camp and said, "This is yours." I lifted my bow and said, "This is mine."

He shook his head and said, "Nothing yours----nothing mine.... just borrowed. Come sit! We will share what is borrowed." He beckoned me and seated me opposite to him. I felt mirth coming from his carefree secure spirit. He reached for a piece of meat and handed it to me. I took it and began to chew. He nodded his head in approval and said, "Meat not mine...not yours. It is a gift."

I became very curious about what this strange warrior expressed and I questioned him, "Tell me about 'not mine...not yours' and 'gifts'".

He laughed and began to tell a tale that enlightened me.

"I shall tell you of gifts; many gifts, much wealth and many things of wonder. My brothers do not see these gifts, but I see."

"This humble one, Happy Hawk, was born into this existence from the warmth of my mother's belly. A very strange existence this is. All things were here when I arrived screaming and kicking from my mother's belly. I had no hair, no teeth, no clothes, and no way to understand even one word. I could not walk, nor hunt nor stand; nor find food. Yet, here I am. I did not bring anything with me, yet everything was provided. Food was provided. Clothes were provided. Shelter was provided, as were eyesight, the sun, the moon, the stars, the trees, the deer and everything else was provided."

He was very animated and jovial as he asked. "Did you bring anything?"

I began to laugh as well for I saw that he was right.

"I did not bring anything either." I replied.

"Isn't that strange? I brought nothing and you brought nothing. Yet you have some fine garments and I have some fine garments. We have food to share even, though; we didn't bring it when we arrived. That is strange isn't it?"

He laughed again. I couldn't argue with this happy one, for his joy was contagious.

"That is very strange, huh?" He prompted me to answer.

"Yes! It is very strange." I replied.

"So, if I didn't bring anything and you didn't bring anything and we came with nothing, how could anything be yours or mine? If anything is yours or mine, then we can take it with us when we leave this life." He laughed again. "Tell me, what are you going to take with you when you leave this life, Huh? Huh? Huh? "

Again he wanted an answer, but I began to laugh. The laughter rolled through me. He had so joyfully expressed a point of much importance. He began to speak again.

"Many of my brothers I have seen leave this existence and do you know what?"

He waited for me to question, "What?"

"Many have I seen who tried to gather up and protect these gifts, to hoard them, to hide them. They fought for them and over them, all the time justifying their actions and yelling, 'IT'S MINE! IT'S MINE!' He shouted the words loud for the whole forest to hear and again he laughed. This laughter came from deep inside him and he rolled on the ground in his glee. His whole body shook.

"But, do you know what?" He continued, "Huh? Huh?"

And again I followed his cue. "What?"

His laughter stopped. Over his features came sadness. He shook his head and said slowly. "All their yelling, all their fighting and all their hoarding was for naught."

He slapped my leg and laughed exuberantly.

"They had to leave it all behind when they left. What a funny joke on them that was, huh?"

I couldn't keep from laughing at the pictures he described for me. He continued, "I have such an easy time. I am so fortunate. Since I don't have anything that is mine, then nothing can be taken from me. I don't have to worry about anyone starting a war with me for my possessions, since I have nothing to fight for. This humble one, in spite of having nothing that is 'mine' has everything. All that I needed the first day out of my mother's belly and all that I need today have been provided. Isn't that strange, huh?" Again, he slapped my leg and laughed.

Yes! I could see this. I could see the joy and the simplicity of this humble one, Happy Hawk. He had accepted a truth that I had never seen before.

"You have given me much of value, Happy Hawk." He interrupted me.

"I give you nothing. You fill my hour with sharing of that which was provided. All is a gift, but not from me. The gift is from the One who provided all things. I own nothing, not even ideas. They were all provided."

I understood then, the deep meaning of his convictions. In gratitude, I shared with Happy Hawk this meeting. We talked of many things way into the night and always he kept insisting on the point that all was a gift. I shared with him my understanding of the gift of the wind and he delighted in the fact that I had learned that truth. We were of one accord as sleep finally overcame us.

As I left the camp the next morning, giving him first my expression of gratitude for the shared gifts, my heart was light. In his joy and simplicity he had achieved a state of being that I could only contemplate. In time, I felt, through finding that which I had been searching for, I would also experience this state of bliss.

I asked myself a question. "If to own means having something that cannot be taken away and, if to have a 'right' is to have an ideal that cannot be taken away, then what is really yours. Strong Elk?" I realized that all my possessions, yes! Even my life, could be taken away. I saw that all these things I "owned" and all the "rights" I had were possessions of a very fragile and precarious quality.

This warrior named Happy Hawk had stated a great truth. There is neither ownership nor rights, but there are many gifts and privileges. I saw that when one assumes something as a possession, whether an 'ideal" or an "object", one tends to take this for granted. One ceases to be vigilant. One then stops putting forth the effort to maintain an awareness of its value. One loses perspective.

But, if one has a gift or has borrowed something of value, if one has a privilege, then one, perhaps, takes care, one pays attention and one preserves the value of it, knowing that it is to be used and experienced as long as it is needed.

This, then, is what Happy Hawk taught me. All things, even life, are a gift. I had not created and not initiated this existence. I had not, in the beginning or many times there-after the ability to survive and, yet, all my needs had been provided. I recognized that an unseen hand had protected me through all my life. A sense of assurance came over me, for I understood that this hand that protected me also guided me to the place where my need could be filled. I saw that in the forests of endless distance, where the meat for sustaining me existed, this hand guided me along the path of the deer that would feed me.

I realized, if I could become more sensitive to this guid-ance, more aware of this force, then, perhaps I would travel faster towards the aim of my existence.

I decided, in the middle of the forest, to offer my song of gratitude for all my gifts and, especially, for the gift of the winds of resistance, for it had made my growth necessary and possible.

CHAPTER 8

THE GIFTS OF THE GREAT HEALER

The Great Healer met me on the trail leading to his village. I had started my journey to find him because his feats of healing had been spoken of often in my village.

I saw a warrior approaching. He was slight of build and younger than I. He was dressed in skins of nearly white and covered with beads of many colors, patterned in beautiful designs. He walked lightly, with an air of confidence about him. Though I had no way of knowing, I knew that this was him who was known as Great Healer, the one I was looking for.

He stopped me as he came near and held up his hand in the sign of welcome. As I responded, he spoke.

"Greetings, though I know not your name, I have waited for you to seek me out."

"I greet you, also, Great Healer." I responded. "I am called Strong Elk. I have come to gain from your wisdom and understanding." I replied.

"So it shall be." He turned around and motioned for me to follow him. We did not again talk until we had entered his lodge and were seated on the robes surrounding the fire.

"Tell me about healing." I requested.

He sat still for several moments, before his words poured forth with much conviction and confidence.

"There is no healing, Strong Elk. There is only an understanding that sickness is a process by which, many times, the body reacts to self inflicted deceit."

My thoughts raced through his words many times, but my mind could not comprehend nor accept this statement. I had no basis of knowledge to deal with it.

I spoke of my understanding so that he might know to which level of awareness I had come.

"Your words are powerful, Great Healer, but they are more powerful than that of the wisdom I have gained in my finding of that for which I was searching. I want to learn your wisdom, but I need it slowly so that I can grasp its meaning in relationship to my experience."

He looked at me and through me. He began to make plain his strong statement in a calm and gentle manner.

"I have come to believe, Strong Elk, through my observations, that there are feelings that man was not meant to have. These feelings, his body cannot cope with over a long period of time. The body reacts to these feelings in a way that is very destructive.

"These feelings which are experienced by all men are very harmful. These feelings are anger, hate, fear, resentment, jealousy, envy, guilt, and insecurity."

"Look back, Strong Elk, at a moment of fear or of anger and see if you can recall how the body reacted."

I did not have to search far, for I understood. I recalled the tenseness, the agitation and the heart beating faster than usual in those moments of anger, fear, resentment and guilt. The Great Healer saw that I understood his words and continued.

"This energy that is created by these feelings is very powerful and the body is only capable of tolerating this energy for a short period of time without harmful effects. This energy is intended to be expended through strong physical action. However, these instances when one is aware of this anger or fear do not happen very often. These feelings that create the sickness are very subtle and very difficult to recognize and acknowledge. The subtle fears; anger, resentments and guilt are of such a slight nature that only one who is truly aware can see them. These subtle feelings come about through fear of disapproval, indifference, inferiority and, only very seldom, from fear of real physical danger or harm. However, once the sickness has been created, by this energy held in from these violent feelings and not allowed to be expressed through action; then the fear of the sickness is added to all the others."

He stopped talking, so I could absorb his understanding. I recalled my battles with the non-persons and the false pictures they had painted in my mind and I recognized, again, all the anxiety that had been present in my life. I was ready to gain the wisdom of the Great Healer.

"When these feelings are accepted without recognition and are held within for long periods of time, the body must adapt to this constant charge of energy."

He stopped again. As we sat in silence, I looked at the reasons for all the feelings that created this energy and I began to speak.

"I have come to accept that all these feelings, of which you speak, come from unfulfilled expectations. The expectations appear to be that of having 'no want' at all levels of existence. Is this the understanding you have as well?"

He smiled and nodded his head and began to speak at a more rapid pace, for he knew we were at the meeting point of awareness.

"This is true. All these feelings come about from unfulfilled expectations or fear of expectations not being realized or expectations of future danger. When an expectation is not realized, one becomes disappointed. When one is disappointed, one feels hurt and looks for something or someone to blame. If the guilty one is seen as someone else, one gets angry. When the one who is held responsible is oneself, one becomes ashamed or guilty. When the blame cannot be easily placed, one becomes fearful and insecure. All these feelings are automatic, or so it seems, once the disappointment has taken place."

"The energy that is created by these feelings must be released. It cannot be contained, for the body has no way of doing this. So the release can come about in many ways. The release can come through violent behavior towards self or others. If it does, then you can understand the reasons for suicide, war, killing and destruction.

"Or the violence goes inside and the body begins to be destroyed by this violence. If it goes inside, it shows up in pain in the belly, pain in the head, in the arms or some other ache.

If this violence continues for a long period of time, the reaction to it finally becomes total and the body dies."

He halted for a moment before continuing. I realized that his powerful statement at the beginning had much validity.

"The healing of the sickness comes, not from me, but it comes from the one who is experiencing the sickness. I provide the tools by which he can begin to stop the self-deceit, so that the feelings that create the sickness do not have the chance to create any violence.

"I work with the sick ones so they are able to see the truth and the grandeur of creation. They begin to recognize that, since without conscious knowledge, there is the ability to create life within the belly of the mother, so there must also be the knowledge to stop the violence against the body. This knowledge comes from finding the source of all creation and following a path of rigorous honesty."

"This honesty you speak of is very elusive and takes much awareness and self-searching to recognize. It is much more and deeper than speaking truthfully so as not to deceive others. What I have come to understand, through my experience, is that any and all things, events, people that are not in the presence and visible to an individual as he takes this breath and heartbeat, at any given moment, is not truth or reality for that individual. It is not the real life. All the thoughts and imaginings about the past or future, whether an hour, a week, a month or years in either direction may have many facts, but the real truth is only in this moment of time."

"Strong Elk, you have seen clearly the most elusive non-truths that man tells himself and others which, in fact, may have more to do with his state of well being and health than anything else. Of course, an individual can experience sickness from starvation or thirst, but many times the sickness comes from another kind of starvation; that being from the health benefits of certain nuts, berries, fruits, vegetables or meat of animals, birds or fish though, perhaps, there is an underlying thought pattern that leads one to excess in certain areas and neglect in other areas. Also, when a person does not participate in physical work or other activities their bodies, over time, will wither and become weak. Also, there are places on this earth that have contaminants towards living forms and the environment is not conducive to health. However, from my observations and experience, much more illness is initiated when a person lives with the anger, guilt, fear, resentments, jealousy, envy towards events or individuals in their past or possibly in the future and these are not physically in the presence of the person suffering from the illness.

"I am sure, I cannot recall all the times I have explained this to individuals and seen them healed when they saw that real life was happening with this breath and this heartbeat. The thoughts, pertaining to another time, place and circumstance, triggered violent emotions and are, in fact, illusions and can lead to delusions which the body will react to as if the events or people are in their presence."

Again, Great Healer stopped to allow me an opportunity to speak.

"Though it took many years for me to see through the illusions I carried in my mind about other times and situation that had been left behind and not happened at all before I came to the recognition you spoke of that NOW is the only place and time of the real life. The stream of thoughts which run through the mind may be facts of what has happened or might happen, however, they are not a part of the truth for this moment. Recognizing this gave me immense freedom. It set me free from anxieties and tensions generated by these self inflicted deceptions which take place when the body is subject to what the mind says is true when it is not focused on the immediate. What is happening now can be verified by our senses: the sense of smell, touch, taste, hearing and sight are always connected to this living moment. A person cannot smell, touch, feel, taste, see or hear tomorrow or yesterday today. Of course, as the power of the non-persons diminished, other senses seem to have been activated, for the mind was not kept busy with irrelevant fantasies and thoughts."

He stopped again to allow for any questions I might have.

"All these things I understand now that you have helped me see them clearly. However, many tales have I heard of your ability to heal instantly sicknesses of a very grave nature. How can this be? If this knowledge, this honesty must be sought out by the sick person, how can the sickness be removed so quickly?"

He explained further.

"Strong Elk, the acts to which you are referring came about after I had been willing to release all the bonds of darkness. I don't know were the gift came from or how. At some point, I realized I had received a gift of oneness with the Source of all things. The Source, through my hands did the healing."

"I cannot show you how to do this instant healing, for it comes not from my wisdom. Perhaps, when you have found the totality of what you have been searching for you will also be given this gift so that you may contribute more fully to life.

"For now, it is sufficient that you have the knowledge to prevent these violences within yourself."

I thanked the Great Healer for his wisdom and we parted. As I returned again to my village I felt very light and safe. I had found more of the wisdom for which I had been seeking.

CHAPTER 9

MEETING WITH THE WISE ONE

Many years had passed since my encounter with THE WISE ONE and many experiences had taught me the value of his understanding. The trail of life had been just as hard and even harder for my people, as we were no match for the power of the colonizers who had descended on our land.

However, the wisdom acquired from using the ideas presented by THE WISE ONE allowed White Fawn and me to be of great support to many of our people.

The wonder of our first time together; after I returned from my journey and the meeting with THE WISE ONE, was etched indelibly into our consciousness. It led us to an acceptance which allowed us to be of great benefit to those who suffered the most and, also, it kept us from taking rash actions that may have led to the total destruction of our people. We learned, acceptance was not the same as resignation and by even submitting, on the surface, to the demands of the conquerors allowed us to preserve our most sacred heritage.

White Fawn had the natural power to see through situations to the underlying truth. She was able to be a comforter to all in need and her words of understanding took much of the sting out of many tragic situations. Many times I heard her ask, when dealing with someone's loss or pain, "What can we do about it now?" This simple question stopped the aggrieved one's thoughts for just an instant.

In that short span of time, she would explain, "When we suffer a wound that bleeds, we let it bleed for a little while and this helps clean the wound. After the initial bleeding, a scab is formed and eventually new skin appears and the scab falls off. If we keep picking at the scab, the wound may never heal and can even turn into a much greater tragedy and cut our lives short."

These were not words she used when a tragedy had just occurred, like the losing of a loved one. At those times she was the ultimate demonstration of love, understanding and compassion. It was only when she saw that the time for healing became prolonged by the individual lingering in the tragedies of the past that she attempted to help them see the harm they were doing to their own lives through allowing the non-persons to have control and maintaining the level of suffering.

Her example of physical healing from a wound or injury gave her the chance to share with them what happens with an emotional injury when the afflicted person keeps on picking at the scab of emotional pain. White Fawn would bring up examples of others in our little band who had suffered tragedies as great and greater than the one she was talking to. She would recount the killing of her brother and mother at the hands of the conquerors, in both cases with no weapons of defense.

She would talk to them of how we both had to accept the facts of the events and how we had to allow our thinking and feelings to go from anger, rage and resentment to forgiveness and gratitude for the fact that we had many memories of sharing and love with those who had passed on. We had to learn to celebrate their lives and their contributions to ours instead of living in the tragedy of their deaths.

These were not easy times for us and, especially for me, Strong Elk. Having been raised as a warrior and a fighter, it was automatic for those non-persons who came forth to be the ones who screamed for vengeance and retribution. It was then that White Fawn's love and understanding led me away from the violent responses to a closer kinship with the Great Spirit. There is no doubt that had I picked up the tools of the warrior and attacked the conquerors with violence. I would have been killed, and the contributions I could have made to our people would have been still-born. It was during this period that I began to learn that the seasons of life will come to us all and that every man and woman will experience gain and loss, tragedy and laughter, sickness and health in the course of their lives and that to ask "What is going on NOW?" in this instant of time, allowed for a re-adjustment of one's thinking and seeing clearly that there was a moment of choice as to whether to accept healing of one's soul or remain in anger, resentment and misery.

Much was learned when, in the middle of a night, after the deaths of White Fawn's mother and brother, the Wise One again appeared to me.

It may have been a dream, for I was lying next to White Fawn and her sleep was not disturbed during our communication.

"Strong Elk," the Wise One began, "you have taken the wisdom I gave you many years ago and become a great asset to your people. You have opened your heart to much and the compassion and love you and White Fawn have demonstrated has given courage to many. This courage has not been the kind that calls for retribution or revenge. It has been the courage to face the truth of situations and the reality of options. It takes much more courage to not fight than it does to fight. Most men do not understand, in the heat of anger and rage; they have submitted to the suggestions of the "non-persons" who, in truth, have only one purpose and that is to destroy the life of the body and mind they occupy."

These were hard words and I was troubled by them. I expressed my concern and confusion and the Wise One went on.

"Think back, Strong Elk, even to the immediate past when the tragedies befell you and White Fawn. In fact, think back into your life and see moments of anger, rage, fear, resentment, envy and all the other feelings that motivated you towards fighting or running. You might see that every suggestion by the "non-persons" led you to internal and external misery and conflict. All of the potential actions of a violent nature seemed, at the time, to be absolutely justified. I ask you, Strong Elk; Who sounded the drums of justification in the beat of justice? Where did the ideas of these violent actions come from?"

I sat silent for a long time, unable to see and understand what the Wise One was attempting to make clear to me.

Presently, he said: "Did not these ideas of rightness and justice come from the images of who you are and those images were, as you have discovered many times, not the real Strong Elk but "non-persons" who were posing as you?"

I did take the time to look back at situations in my life that brought out the non-persons and the havoc which ensued when I allowed their suggestions to control my actions. I spoke from the depths of my being when I said to THE WISE ONE:

"Much injustice has been done to my people, to White Fawn and to me and turning away from revenge is not something that comes natural to me. The actions of the conquerors have been so heinous and the destruction so devastating to the tribes of Turtle Island that retribution is demanded."

I was choking back the anger and my words were filled with vitriol.

"Wise One, I have followed the trail that was laid out in our first meeting and it has been a blessing to me, to White Fawn and as well to many in our band. What has happened to our people must not be allowed if I, Strong Elk, am to survive as a man and a warrior. If a man and a warrior cannot come to the defense of the defenseless, how can he possibly live with himself? I ask you, Wise One; " How can I possibly live with myself if I do not give to the conquerors like for like?"'

Never, before or after have I experienced such inner pain. All of me screamed for revenge and justice. I looked into the eyes of the Wise One and saw sadness, pain and compassion. We sat silently for many long moments before he again spoke to me.

"Strong Elk, what you say and the way that you feel at this moment is your truth and it is not wrong. You have lived for years attempting to instill the concept of justice in your people. You have spoken to many a warrior in an attempt to advance the idea that strength, without a concept of fairness and justice is animal brutality.

"Now, your people have been attacked by those who have strength of force and weapons beyond those available to you and your people, however, they do not have the character of spirit or morality to have adopted ideas of compassion and understanding. They do not have the wisdom to see that what their acts are doing is destroying the very foundations of their souls. The law of conquering the weak, the infirm, the gentle is not a sign of being a man or a human. It is the sign instead of a soul-sickness that has taken control of a large portion of the conquerors. Many have seen that they talk with forked tongues, speaking of peace, love, brotherhood while planning the destruction of gentle and peaceful peoples.

"However, Strong Elk, even the idea of justice, in these times, is not sufficient to erase what has fallen upon your people. Another level of being must come about for you and your people to survive this period and carry them forward to a time when a higher order of thinking has dissolved the feelings which are now prevalent."

I could not understand what the Wise One was referring to and how these feelings of rage could dissolve. When he saw the mixture of pain and rage etched on my face and in my eyes, he continued.

"Strong Elk, violence begets violence. This has been the history of mankind, once the concept of justice, as it is practiced, was accepted by man. It was better, for sure, than the law of strength over weakness and survival of the stronger and destruction, death or slavery for the weaker. Very few would disagree with the idea of retribution for pains inflicted, however, I want you to consider another option for you; an option that does not take away from your manhood, does not involve killing to compensate for lives that have been taken and may lift you to a higher understanding and preserve the lives of your people so that generations can go on living.

"Understand, Strong Elk: No one who knows you could ever question your courage or your manhood. Long before I came to council you, your reputation as a warrior of courage and strength was established and, now, with many years having passed; wisdom, compassion and insight has been added to that mix. I want to make sure you understand what I am saying now. There is a better way than killing for killings sake and a better way than the law of justice. Perhaps, at this time only a few individuals are prepared and capable of going beyond what has been accepted as a way to deal with conflict, however, you are one of those who may be able to. I am not telling you that you must. I am telling you that you may be willing to go beyond the levels that other warriors and wise men are willing to; and most of the conquerors are absolutely incapable of."

Somehow, while the Wise One was talking to me, the violent feelings I had experienced were dissipating and the rage had subsided, so that I could listen to his council. I do not know how this came about, but it must have been transference of the peace of the Wise One, for I wanted to know a better way to live life than through violence and conflict.

"Only the truly strong can go beyond force and violence, Strong Elk, to understanding and compassion. Only those few who see through all the illusions of power and into the heart of those who use it to try to still their fears, can grasp the path that I am talking about. The more a man lives in fear, the more he wants power so he can conquer his fears and vanquish those who are not willing to submit to his dictates. Such a one is not a man, in any sense of the word, and he certainly has not reached the level of being a human being. I am sure, by now, you are wondering what I am trying to get you to understand. It is not easy to put into words. One who is truly strong is one who has seen that but for a certain grace, he could have fallen into the same kind of actions that are displayed by the conquerors. One who is truly strong, knows in his heart of hearts that at many moments of his life, a different action could have been taken that led to tragedies of a grave nature for him and others. Only a certain grace allowed him to maintain his humanity.

"So, I ask you, Strong Elk, to weigh the action of vengeance and you being killed, while protecting the image of being a warrior, against you staying alive and sharing the love and wisdom that is in you with your people. For, surely, you will be hunted down and killed. The conquerors have the power of numbers and better weapons and are not hampered neither by love, compassion or conscience. So, the death songs will be sung over you and the image of the brave warrior will survive while you, Strong Elk, who hold in your hands the wisdom and the tools to help your people survive and maintain the contact and reverence for our Earth Mother will be no more. You will have thrown away your life and left your people to face many tragedies without your wisdom, strength and courage to guide them."

I was truly stunned by the Wise One's reasoning for the bile of revenge had been present and screaming for me to protect the image of the great warrior. It was easy to see, at that moment, that to acquiesce to the Wise One's council would require much more courage than to attack, as the warrior image of the "non-persons" required, and die in battle.

I was still for a long time as I sorted through my feelings and thoughts.

Presently, I spoke, "Wise One, I hear you and understand what you have tried to give me of your wisdom and your council. I even agree with you, however, I must tell you the truth and that is, I do not know if I have the strength and courage to take the course you have laid out for me. I have worked hard to reduce and eliminate the power of the "non-persons", however, in this instance, the voices are shouting at me with such force that to maintain control seems almost beyond human ability. It is as if the courage needed to live is much greater than the courage to sacrifice my life in battle, knowing that I will be honored and remembered for that, while choosing to follow your council will leave me, Strong Elk, open to ridicule and accusations of cowardice."

The pain I was feeling was so deep and palpable that I could not go on speaking. My head was downcast as I was unable to focus on a single thought and the waves of violent emotions were washing over me. In absolute desperation I screamed, "How can I get the strength to accept and act on your council?"

When I looked up, the Wise One was gone and I was left alone to ponder the event that had just taken place.

CHAPTER 10

WHITE FAWN'S GIFTS

As I lay there with the thoughts of the Wise One's admonitions running through my head, White Fawn stirred and moved close to me. She murmured, "Are you awake, Strong Elk?" I told her I was and she asked what had awakened me. I told her about the dream and the conversation with the Wise One. Though still in a sleep state she came awake and asked, "Do you need to talk about this, Strong Elk?"

Through the years, she had become my greatest councilor and confidant. Her insights had helped me weather many storms and given me points of view that allowed me to overcome many obstacles and potential conflicts. When I saw that she was fully awake, I retold the whole story of this contact with the Wise One, leaving nothing out and including the fears and angers I experienced when it became clear that to live, without taking the action of the warrior, would be harder than anything I had ever done. Yet to allow the conquerors to kill me in battle could, as the Wise One intimated, deny our people the guidance and council necessary to survive and, perhaps, one day return to the ways of our forefathers.

White Fawn listened in silence while her head rested upon my chest and her gentle hand lay lightly on my breast. After hearing the whole tale and considering all its implications, she spoke in the calm and measured way which had always soothed my spirit when I was troubled.

"The council you have been given is wise, Strong Elk, and it behooves you to look at it deeply before you decide on an action. I am your wife and have been with you in my heart since before the first time we met. I have known the real you and know the truth of who you are, the courage you have and the compassion and love you have for me and our people. It breaks my heart to see and feel the turmoil in your soul.

"You have taught me, as well as many others, the traps that are set by the "non-persons" and how their only purpose is to spread conflict and, in the end, destroy the living man or woman. When you choose to go their way, there are many who will honor you for actions that may destroy our people, yet save the face of the image the "non-persons" want to save.

"As you have said, it is much harder to follow the path of putting aside the anger and hate the "non-persons" want you to act on and, in many cases, experience the ridicule and derision of those who are blind to the reality and truth of the situation.

"What I want you to know is that with all my heart and, I believe, the hearts of our people, you are valued and respected above all others and that you are, in fact, the only one with the wisdom and strength to carry us through and inspire us in these times. I am sure the Great Spirit would rather have you alive, though humbled by the act of putting the interest and survival of our people ahead of the image of the warrior, and thereby fulfill a much greater function for our people."

"Yes! My husband, a part of my feelings are those of self-ishness because I cannot stand the thought of loosing you and you have always given me the wisdom, strength and love to go on when my heart has been broken and my spirit has been brought low. But, more important than that, I feel together we have represented the unity that has and will continue to give hope and courage to others."

"We, truly, are much stronger when we work in harmony with a common purpose than either one of us could be on our own. The challenge for our people now is so enormous that I can't help but feel our example of courage and unity is required above all else to lift them up and sustain them."

I couldn't help being touched by her calmness and her clarity in pointing out the path I had to choose. Perhaps, the only reason I was willing to forego the demands of the warrior image was the deep knowledge that to do otherwise would be to negate all the ideas I had presented to our people in a self-ish act of trying to sustain the image of the warrior. I knew that White Fawn had, through our years together, become an inseparable part of me and the wisest mate a man could have.

"White Fawn, I cannot be successful in being a guide to our people without your help and council. You are the part of me that leads me to re-think my actions and their consequences and you have always given me insights which lift my spirit to see possibilities beyond those of the warrior. So, as you are willing to be by my side and be unflinching in your support, I am willing to take this path that might lead to condemnation and accusation of cowardice. You have helped me see, along with the Wise One; there are choices that demand one to make decisions and take actions for the greater good than to sustain the self-images the "non-persons" want preserved."

I felt her tears on my chest as I heard her soft voice express her deep gratitude for the choice I had made.

"My husband, it is such a great gift to me to know that together we are in harmony in our purpose to take the tragedies that has befallen us and be lifted above them. It confirms all I have known and felt about you and us. We truly are blessed to have a great purpose for our lives above our personal desires and comfort. I thank you and I love you."

Yes! As had happened so many times through our years together, even now with the tragedies greater than we had ever experienced, we both knew that our hearts were beating to the same rhythm and it gave us both strength.

CHAPTER 11

WHITE FAWN

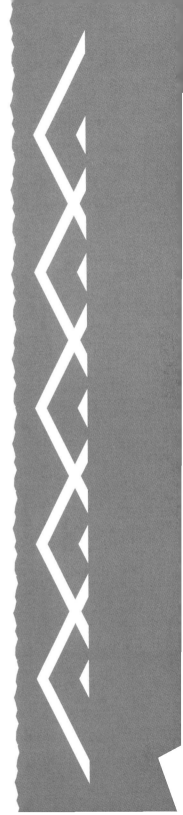

"Strong Elk, please tell our story to all who will listen."
I had been sitting with White Fawn for several days as I saw her getting weaker and weaker. The years we had supported each other had been many and there was much of value to be shared. "I had a dream." She said weakly as she reached for my hand and squeezed it. "The dream was very beautiful and peaceful. I know that it is close to the time when I must leave you but do not be sad.

"We lived a life so rich in the understanding that you brought to us and our people and it must be shared. This is what the dream was about."

She closed her eyes and I waited for her to speak again. My love for her and for the gifts we had shared became very vivid. The many years we had shared were so filled with all that make up a rich life. We had been blessed to have been given the tools to lift us above the events of life and to see a pattern in the rug that we wove. Yes! Midst all the joy and fulfillment had been many severe tragedies, yet they had made our bonds stronger and our love and compassion for our fellows deeper. Sitting next to her during these last days had made me realize how incredibly fortunate I had been to have a wife whose every act and thought blended with the purpose we had chosen so many years before. I, Strong Elk, had acknowledged; it would have been impossible for me to have survived, as a human being, had it not been for White Fawn's gentle council and love. There had been times when the non-persons of my youth would have led me into battles I could not have survived, yet, with her at my side, she gave me the strength to surrender the path of war, disharmony and fear and choose, instead, the path of compassion, love and understanding. She stirred and her eyes opened.

"What a joy it has been to walk these many miles with you and to breathe in the wonder of creation. Without your insights and wisdom, I would never have known the richness that life can bestow on anyone, even amidst the most violent storms. My husband, you gave us a way of living in a reality that most humans may never understand or be willing to commit to. What a blessing you have been to me and to so many others through the years. That is why I want you to tell our story, to make humans understand that there is a better way then the one presented by the revered ones, a better way than the ones presented by the non-persons of our own creation, a better way than living in fear, anger, jealousy, hate, resentments."

It took White Fawn a long time to express these words for she was very weak. She would drift off, for several minutes at a time, while relating these feelings to me and she would squeeze my hand to let me know that she was not finished.

"The dream told me that our life has made a difference, Strong Elk, and our journey has given much encouragement and hope to those who came into our lives and saw and felt the wonder of living in the understanding that you presented. So many times, I felt, if there was a way for you to become many; peace and love would be multiplied many times over. So, my husband, I want you to tell the story and it is my prayer that enough of those who hear it will live in the understanding and become examples for others so that, like a ripple going out in the pond after a stone has been dropped into it, a new reality will emerge for many people."

"White Fawn, none of what our life has been could have happened without you being there to give me courage and strength and many times to lead the way. Without you, how can I possibly be able to present the totality of the wonders that have been ours to share?"

"Strong Elk, if you sit there quietly without thought, for a moment or two, you will feel in your heart that I will never leave you. Perhaps my body will not be present, but as you have experienced with the Wise One, at any time you will be able to close your eyes and reflect on me and I will be there for you to give you strength and support. When we live in the love we have learned to accept and express, there is no separation for we are truly one with all of creation and of each other. You don't have to believe this, Strong Elk, for as, with all the other learning we have had, you will experience it."

Again, silence surrounded us, yet in my heart I could feel what she had just put into words. I closed my eyes and saw her standing there before me, the beautiful young maiden as we became man and wife. I could hear her laughter and feel her excitement and joy as our journey together began. It would be natural for me to feel that my heart was breaking as she was slowly slipping from this life, however, as I reflected on our life together I was filled with the awesome gratitude, trust and love that had sustained me through so many difficult times. It was as if White Fawn was guiding my thoughts and feelings and letting me know that we were one and would be one, even after her passing. Words cannot describe the richness of the moment. And, as her breathing slowly faded, I uttered words of truth that must have been echoed by White Fawn, words that I had first become familiar with during the meeting with Happy Hawk. "Great Spirit!, Thank you for having loaned White Fawn and me to each other for all these many years. My gratitude is unbounded for the fullness that our life together has been." Yes! Immense sadness touched me, but in my heart I felt her letting me know that she would always be with me and that I would not be alone.

I continued to sit with her for a long time and allowed her last words to repeat themselves in my mind and to, silently, commit myself to honoring her last request. So, I will tell the story she wanted me to tell.

CHAPTER 12

THE FEELING WHICH IS

Through my finding that which I, Strong Elk, had been searching for a state of being, a new consciousness, a feeling which is always present came about. This feeling which is, cannot be described in words. This feeling which is, must be experienced to be known. This feeling which is, begins to come about with the willingness to find. The path to finding is simple, but being simple does not imply that it is easy. The journey, at times, can be very painful. It takes courage and perseverance to continue, but this pain will pass. The pain will last only as long as the one who is finding is unwilling to see. This then has been the story of my journey. It began with a need. It began with a willingness to look within, a willingness to find and separate the non-persons from the one within. The willingness to see that beneath all the Strong Elks that I had created was a different Strong Elk from the one I had allowed the world to see. I further came to recognize that I did not own and did not have rights. However, I had many privileges and gifts for which to be thankful. I understood that the greatest gift of all, next to life itself, was the gift of the wind of resistance that prodded and prompted me to grow. I began to recognize an unseen hand protecting me and guiding me towards that which was of need to me....to the winds that would allow me to soar towards my destiny, towards those things that would awaken me from my walking slumber.

The realization that there was a protecting hand, a guiding hand that knew my needs before I could express them in words, removed my fears. At this point in my journey, an understanding came about, an understanding that there is a larger aim then the aim of "no want". This aim is to grow. An understanding that to grow strong there must be the wind of resistance, an understanding that every act of all my brothers, of all my enemies, of all who touched me and of myself, Strong Elk, were thought to be the proper and just act of the moment, in the light of the awareness of the one doing it. An understanding that each man has within the one who wants to do no harm, who wants to be considerate and wants to make a contribution to life. But, this one within has been trampled on by all the "non-persons" to the point where he is hidden from the world.

An understanding came to me that only I, Strong Elk, am responsible for my inner feelings and that all is as it must be at any given moment in time. Through this process of looking within, I realized that all is a gift and arriving at the state of understanding, it became necessary to take action. I, Strong Elk, had to acknowledge to my innermost self that I had been and was nothing. I had allowed all the "non-persons" in my life to rule my life and these "non-persons" had led me to do much harm, create much confusion and make life around me one of turmoil. I admitted to my innermost self that what I had projected to my brothers and my world as being Strong Elk was an untruth, in fact there were many untruths. After receiving this understanding, it became my need to relinquish and give up.

What did I give up and surrender? I gave up and set free from my mind all the "non-persons" who were "not I" but who posed as me for the world to see. I gave up the conclusion of the little one that the whole purpose and the only aim in life were to have "no wants". I gave up the conclusion of having the "right" to no pain, no disapproval, and no indifference. I relinquished the idea and ideals of the little and all the non-persons who had been created by me to protect me from a world I did not understand. I, Strong Elk, then turned away from the aim of the little one and the "non-persons" and I began to walk on a different path towards a different aim. This aim was to experience all of life and to grow. I began to be thankful and appreciate the winds of resistance in all its many forms for they were of great value in helping my ascent towards my new aim. I began to be grateful for the things from which I had previously struggled to escape. I began to see from a different set of values, the values of the one within who wanted to be considerate, harmless and to make a contribution to life. I, Strong Elk, began to respond to the gifts of life, moment to moment with laughter in my heart. The strings of the puppet had been cut.

I do not know how or when it took place, but one moment I realized that something had left me. I found that the violent feelings, the turmoil and the confusion were no longer present. It was as if anger, fear, jealousy, envy, guilt, resentment, hate, insecurity and despair had been washed from my being. The feeling "which is" was what remained. This feeling which is can be experienced when everything else has been washed away.

I know that every man can experience this feeling which is, this state of being that is beyond the description of words. It only takes a willingness to find who one really is beneath all the masks and costumes of the "non-persons". It is the hope of White Fawn and I that our contribution will lead you towards experiencing the feeling "which is" and the journey will be filled with the wonderment of creation.

The End

ARTIST'S PROFILE

Steinar, a self described "wanderer", was born in Norway and began his quest for knowledge on a freighter plying the cargo route around South America at the age of sixteen. The initial adventure gave him a foretaste of a life that led him through many countries; dozens of major careers(as he puts it), including commercial fishing, restaurateur, salesman, service station operator and, finally, at age 47 settling on art as a vocation and writing as an avocation. Parts of THE GIFT OF THE WIND were written, in 1976, when he woke up from a dream about "the one traveling on the path of non-forgiveness". This led him to begin, in earnest, the journey of self-discovery and inner searching. Many copies of the manuscript were given out to friends, along the way, who were in need of the information it contained. However, he always felt that if THE GIFT OF THE WIND was to become a published book it needed to be illustrated. Though, he had become an accomplished self-taught painter, while recovering from an auto accident that required two back surgeries and years of recuperation, somehow the images did not come to him until much later, after he had begun sculpting. The cover photo is of his depiction of Strong Elk, carved in Black Walnut. When, finally, he was prompted by a shaman, in Central Mexico, to expose the writing to a larger audience he became willing to do so. The images that came to him were created and he was able to complete the book and make it ready for publication. As a result of going deeply into the creative process for the sculptural pieces, he experienced many insights that saw THE GIFT OF THE WIND TRILOGY as a reality and this has become his focus. He has much written on PART II and PART III and is spending time in a small Indian village in Central Mexico while finishing the writing. Still on the shelf is a yet to be published novel in English and an unfinished murder mystery in Norwegian.

For more information on Steinar's
Art, go to the website
www.giftofthewind.com

WHAT READERS SAY

"The Gift of the Wind" was wonderful reading. You dun good. I particularly enjoyed Chapter 2, the forgiving and the freeing of the spirit and superficial judgments. Strong Elk dealt with the suicide of the nice self, and yet found a certain amount of grief essential for future growth. Did he allow a bolt of pain to strike? Yes, because it was useful pain; lightning illuminates. Pain had become something more valuable: experience. Strong Elk stood knee-deep in the flow of life and paying close attention, he found peace, courage and humility. The poet William Meredith has observed that the worst that can be said of a man is the "he did not pay attention." White Fawn paid attention and so did Strong Elk. Steinar, you have been blessed with the gift of writing. Keep using your talents and your abilities to make the world a better place."
Teresa   — Orr, MN

"I was presented with a copy of the "Gift of the Wind" by Steinar in Yelapa Mexico at a time of extreme change in my life. I found the story to be a consuming validation for and of life. It was incredible the way the energy pulled me in to the story and I felt as though I became this story. I felt a change wash over me subtle yet clear which has now become apart of my life, the life of a creator, an artist, that which I have always been and again in the process of being.

As one who is redefining his life, I recommend the "Gift of The Wind" as a potential stepping stone for any one seeking change, wisdom and understanding."

— Tom Duke — Artist/Creator, Sammamish, WA

"My soul will never be the same after reading "The Gift of the Wind". You simply touched a part of my inner core and illuminated it with light and love, and truth."

— Ginny, , CT

"Put on the new moccasins offered by the Gift of the Wind and you just may find yourself stepping over the worn out paradigms of instant gratification and the gobbling of personal power (control and dominance.) The gifts found here, when utilized, will lift the seeker toward the life that one always thought possible. There is peace in these pages (or, the consciousness behind these pages is Peace)."

— Bill Loewen, jd, self-imortan author of Prayers for Pop, to be published if written-maybe Phoenix, AZ

Steinar Karlsen finds a way to approach significant spiritual concepts in a user friendly manner through his conversational storytelling style. His protagonist, Strong Elk, tells of encounters with spirits, animals, a shaman, his wife, his tribe, that have resulted in deep understanding of issues like judgment, peace, surrender, staying in the moment, getting beyond ego, respect, honor, acceptance, gratitude and True Love = the biggies. Personally, I really enjoyed that Steinar chose the Native American setting for his stories as I feel their tribal lifestyle exemplifies these important lessons.

As a spiritual teacher, I welcome this work that creates a bridge to approach profound concepts that many have felt were unapproachable. It is a quick read yet delivers depth.

— Carol Heywood-Babrauskas, Author Preston, WA
Passionate Pinky and the Evolutionary Experiment www.passionatepinky.com

---

I just finished your book and enjoyed it, immensely. The messages in each story were great and I find them affecting me directly as I walk my own path to reason and sanity. As you know there have been several trials in my life as of late and the stories have provided me with plenty to reflect on as I move forward in this latest quest. Thank you for the opportunity to read this and allowing my input.

— Mark Mc Kinney, Seattle, WA

Foreward by William Loewen, jd:

"Within each individual is a spark waiting to be fanned into the flame of a new life. The Gift of the Wind is the fresh breeze that accomplished just that on my own personal journey into freedom. This new, yet timeless story will touch your heart and heal your vision to see Life as a beautiful dawning, an unfolding of the Infinite that it is."here, when utilized, will lift the seeker toward the life that one always thought possible. There is peace in these pages (or, the consciousness behind these pages is Peace)."

AUTHOR'S GRATITUDE LIST

Many people contributed to the publishing of this book with their support and insights. The one standing at the top of the list is Dr. Robert Gibson who, as is said these days, walked his talk and inspired untold others to do the same. Lana Nunn, whose friendship through thirty years, was always cheerfully supportive. Bill Loewen, who, twenty eight years ago, was the first to take the information in The Gift of the Wind and let it move him to a new life purpose. Johnny Howard, a man of boundless compassion and wisdom, who has followed my meanderings for many years. Jimmie Blackfeather, over coffee at the Grand Hotel on the square in Patzcuaro, Mexico, insisted that the book needed to be published. I give a special thanks to my daughters, Cindy and Kayleen, who accepts this vagabond and embraces his adventures with enthusiasm and love. My grandson Lincoln, a young man with the heart of gold and the courage of a Viking, inspires me more than he knows; Ross Bell, who opened my mind to the wonders of man, books and ideas as I cleaned his bakery at night while finishing high-school; Henry Littlfield, native American, fisherman and mayor of Metlakatla, Alaska when I worked on his boat in 1959: What I learned in one short season, among his people and with his insights, was material for many books. Reverend Johnson, the black minister and WWII veteran who was in the same room with me at Mountain View Hospital, in Tacoma, Washington, while recovering from diagnosed TB. His calmness and faith guided me through the incredible fear that gripped me during this period of my life. Kales Lowe, attorney and Federal Judge, who embraced me like the son he never had, led me through the intricacies of the law and the political system to see, perhaps more than a young idealistic young man should. My parents, Astrid and Einar, whose blood flows through the veins of me, my sisters and our progeny and who demonstrated the infinite capacities to overcome adversity and fill our lives with appreciation, accomplishments and laughter. There are many more, in many countries, cultures and ethnicities who have given of themselves so that my heart and soul have been filled to overflowing with joy, peace, love and serenity. They were examples all of the incredible brotherhood of man that transcends religion, nationalism, politics and isolationist notions of superiority. My gratitude to you for the spice, flavor, color and texture you gave to my life is unbounded. Thank you.